Xoxo, Your Psycho Ex-Lover

Sheila Martinez

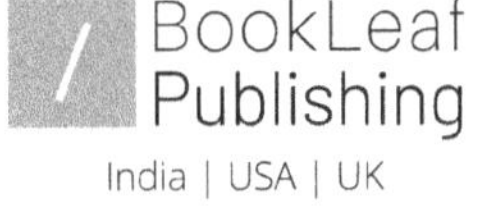

BookLeaf Publishing

India | USA | UK

Presentation by *BookLeaf Publishing*

Web: www.bookleafpub.com

E-mail: info@bookleafpub.com

ISBN: 9789363315808

First edition 2024

The Saddest Souls

You thought of me and I envied her
We found ourselves tangled, our hands tied
Cling to me like your last lifeline
I promise to follow suit
Drown us in a sea of beer
Engulfed in each other's sadness
Enriched with each other's madness
Intertwine our dreams
And let a sweet delusion take root
My heart was weeping long before we
met
You redirected the tears, but our hearts
were doomed to be tortured
The saddest souls, in the darkest room
of hole-filled walls
We existed to hold on to each other
To bridge the sorrow and feel a spark of life
If only for a season, a moment, a feeling in time
But a safety net cannot work both ways
And so we watched it fray
Thread by thread, teardrop by teardrop
We lost a part of us that was never meant to be, a
part of our story they wouldn't believe
Our unpublished story that no one got to read
I'll meet you anywhere.. Just say when

I'll give in to our toxic cycle of love and anguish
But only long enough to climb from our
darkness and leave you to fade into a tender
memory
A sore spot of healing
I force myself to burn the final fibers of my once
beloved safety net

Where's the Thrill

I watched you pace around like the floorboards
would last an eon
Like your persistent pattern wouldn't wear on the
very thing supporting you
You're my new addiction
To everything bad that made me feel good
Late nights and screaming fights
I'd walk miles to get away
But where's the thrill if there's nothing to chase?
So let's play this game
Until the death we would duel
But you failed to read me your self-serving rules
My arms shimmer with the most loving shades
of amethyst

I know it was an accident, right?
Your army's loyalty now resides with me
They flock to protect the damsel stuck in
daydreams
To pave an escape route with ease
A council of warnings I couldn't accept
I was battered but alive
With you, I was so alive
Young enough to be swayed and swooned by
anything new
Reckless enough to allow destruction by you
I can still feel the heat of your blue-eyed glare
The way you'd shake your head at my city ways
But I'd give my pound of flesh for you to stay
And you'd so greedily welcome it
This flesh was yours after all
A clean wild canvas of laughter and life
dedicated to you
I'll drive hours just for a half-hearted embrace
I'll sing and dance and play your games
From one apartment to the next
Until all the floorboards are worn down to
splinters in my feet
Until I crawl far enough away so your
hollowness can't reach me
I know I'll learn to stand again and begin to
rebuild my world
It's devastating that I can't say the same for your
next girl

White Pine

I fell for you
Whatever that meant at the time
Doodles of our names
Girly, nostalgic, cliche
Yet to learn that you wouldn't be mine
Too young to understand the hurt
Scandalous meeting of our lips
I told my friends that I'd be fine
It's ok you didn't choose me
But still... I fell for you
So maybe we were never lovers
Maybe we were only 12
The lesson remains the same
Unrequited and misunderstood feelings
The harshness of a blonde-haired boy
Who never meant to hurt anyone
Tell me you'll stay sweet
That we will meet in a local bar in our 20s
You'll apologize for what happened when we
were kids
I'll smile and brush it off
Like I never thought about that first lesson in
love
Like it didn't pave a path to fighting for my
lover's attention more than I should

I hope it doesn't haunt you
Hurting the young feelings of a brown-eyed girl
who found magic in your smile
A football-shaped note away from being yours
I think of you like a mixed CD playing on a
school bus
Skipping on my Walkman everytime we hit a
bump
You are memories of running free and learning
who to be
I'm lucky to have known you then
And I hope life has been nothing but kind
But if I'm being honest
I hope that sometimes you think about how you
could've been mine

Stained

I begged you to love me
I needed you to love me
If there was no you, how could there be a me
All I could see was you, all I could feel was you
And yet you lined our conversations with
excuses for us not to be
But I can prove to you I'm the one
I can show you how perfect I can be
Muffle my cries into a pillow alone at night
Holding onto hope that you'll reach back out to
me
When you did, your words were cruel
But I love you, I need you
I'll remain steadfast in my desperation to be
loved by you
I'll table all concerns I can see so clearly could
be the end of future us
I'll give you all that I have and all that I am
And so I offered up my throat and threw caution
to the wind
I didn't even notice the pain when you drew my
blood
It seeped onto my skin and left stains for me to
proudly cover with my clothes and defenses

A perfect crime of a willing victim waiting to be
slaughtered
You say you didn't realize the creature you had
become
But that won't replace the blood drained from
my veins
That won't close the wounds I now bare
All of which seem practically self-inflicted
But I loved you... I needed you

Let's Rage

It doesn't look too far down from these old
shingles
I can see beyond the treeline
Smell the burning fire surrounded by you and
your friends
Seemingly taunting my tempted tragedy
I'm alone within the walls of what I call home
Not in control of the acidic tears dripping down
my cheeks
I can hear you trying to silence me
Lock me in a tower with no way out but this
window
Like a wildfire, my despair turned to rage
An old curtain rod and a room full of moving
boxes never stood a chance
Swing once because of your lies

Swing twice because you made me feel so small,
An insignificant existence
Swing again because you blamed me for
everything
You tarnished my good intentions
Made me feel like I alone was the problem
Isolated me
Hated and berated and ran me out of town
Never expected to be where I am now
A beautiful little room claimed by my
annihilation
You were my best friend
You were supposed to have my back
Swing, smash and utterly trash this room
Screaming with my soul into another dimension
Perspective and strength paired with my brutal
truths
This rage came to save my life
I shattered glass into pieces
Assorted in a single beam of sunlight on this
floor
Reflecting like stardust onto the walls that will
always know the cyclone I'm capable of
I hear the curtain rod hit the floor by my side
I make a path through my demolition
Bloody hands and angry tears can be wiped
clean
But I will be forever changed
I will forever know the strength of my rage

Up In Smoke

I can time your calls
Like the shadow on a sundial
You ring and I ignore
Just one more chance you hastily implore
Like you weren't the one to light us ablaze
But from our coals
I became something new
My scars are proof of my healing
My mental escape from a rogue beggar
New tricks and masks stock my armory
You no longer have a stake in me
I reroute and reroot
And grow into a hemlock grove
My words like poison
Slowly setting in
Reminding you of what we should've been
There is no place left for you here
Pack up your regret
It's all you have left
A tragic decree of how you lost me
Day in, day out
You refused to understand
The little things I found suffocating
Can you even recognize me now
My beautiful smile replaced with a grin

My flinchless stance against your charge
I dare you to cross this heart that's now barbed
Seemingly careless and quick to snap
I'll shred your romantic sentiments
And meet your words with an attack
Funny you think one chance will work
When you've had thousands daily
You abused with a smirk
Go ahead and call me mean
I am what you made me
Just your mirroring smoke screen

Double Text

What's a hotel room between acquaintanced
strangers
I'd surrender my key for a night of getting to
know you
To break the intimidation
Muddy our situation
And simply open a door
Your gentle way with words nudges me to go
mad
The slippery slope of my mind has me in a
chokehold
How could we possibly suppress this?

I'd flood my thoughts with anything else but you
if I was strong enough
But the high tides make for a wild ride of
moving on
The pull you have on me
The intrigue you spark in me
I'm captive to overthinking, underspeaking,
hardly breathing
I want to call, double text and just obsess
I like the way you steal my mind
I like the way this hurts
Don't let me lose your attention
Or let me be too much
So I'll step back and hold my tongue
Until you say it's fine
Until the day you recognize my soul from
another life
Now I'm tied to you so I'll confide in you
I'll hide myself less, wrapped in radical honesty
Your permissive personality and my eternal
positivity
Were destined to collide
A lightning strike at the perfect time
Let's take over the world
Will you hold my hand, no
Come lay by my side
Make sure these dreams of mine never die

# Devastation In the Dark

Some nights just aren't dark enough
I wasn't made to be a sad soul
But maybe without you I am
Maybe because of you I am
I can't organize my thoughts enough to decipher
all that I'm buried under
An emotionless cry that will never reach the ears
of another
This cloud isn't thick enough to take me away
Stop this pain
Make sure my porcelain smile will never see the
light of another day
What's to become of my howling heart?

It's been maimed and shredded, torn thoroughly
apart
An abrupt halt, dissociated distortion
But they would never know
I reach out and reach in, more empty-handed
than ever
We bleed differently, you and I
My porous skin making way for spouts of grief
Weeping bandages with rotting flesh underneath
Planted poppies attempt to cover the wounds
But even beautiful things reflect the death of this
youth
This liberation is devastation in the dark
And I alone have to heal this heart

Busy Worker Bee

You built me up to believe I was invincible
Against everything and everyone but you
I was special and strong and encouraged
As long as it suited you
And so I defended you endlessly
I let you let me down, your perpetual prey
I used love as an excuse to make it okay
Until the day I stopped
So now I'll reinvent every surface of this house
Every edge of my shattered being
Every wall, shelf, thought, and bad habit
I'll cover it all in a new shade of paint
Adorned with trinkets and a side of
pharmaceutical support
After all, busy is the best thing I know how to be
Busy is the only thing that makes me, me
I plan and research and recruit some friends
But it's only me staying up still painting at 10
I chase a productive high to keep my mind off
you
To keep me focused and happy
So I don't always have to think of what we went
through
It feels good to be busy
To feed my creative mind

I'll keep making beautiful spaces
Until it's simply a beautiful life

Set In Ink

Do you want to get a tattoo?
Let's stay wild and young
Instill in my mind what love is meant to be
How passion was designed
Lead me to get lost in the essence of your soul
A passage to forever
Earth spun until it nudged me to you
A gesture of fate made true
A connection we can't undo
Turn me into something just yours
A sacred place, a timeless touch
I need to know your overwhelming love
Trace my lips and guide my hips
Brand me to my core
Our bodies are our trademark
Extending through each life
I feel I must have known you
At least a million times
I wonder, of all the chances we're given
How many did we get this right?
I won't survive without your hand in mine
Our fingers woven together
Reflecting our intimacy
I feel you ever so slightly starting to let me go
You guide me to the tallest peak

For me to jump alone
I'll still wait for you once I hit the bottom
With all my shattered bones
A passion I thought could never fade
Paralyzes me in the haunting bed that we made
You'll keep coming back around
Like a pattern I can't escape
Echoing 3-3-3
A message to the us we are meant to be
I'll etch it in stone for all the twin flames yet to
come
Pleading to learn from our glittering ashes
Ignite your match and keep close guard
It's a gift and curse to love this hard

Is It Me?

I'm always wrong
The way you put me down
A vile legacy of a man
You seal me away from everything I adore
From everything I know in this sparkling world
Force my hand to be your slave
And I still love you at the end of the day
Your power over my emotion
Seems to be what rules your kingdom
And the moat you built to hide me away
Made it so I couldn't run
You steal my voice
And wrong my rights
You took away my fire to fight
I'm helpless and hungry
Starving for your attention
Trembling for your affection
But maybe I'm the one who poured this
foundation
Enabled all of your tormenting actions
Finding it simple to point the finger
My most intoxicating role
The vixen enthralled to be the victim
I'll twist your words

To make you see how it's you who's always
wrong
My people pleasing, self-righteous breathing
Helps to lead to my demise
Because I projected my pain on you
Self-victimizing almost claimed my life

My Side of the Coin

From your side of the coin
I'm always thoughtful ever giving
Sweet and kind with a life worth living
And I am
But my oceans expand much deeper
I'm lonely and humbled every time you fail to
respond
Love-soaked memories fill my head
They keep me holding on
I'm here for you, I chant and cheer
But who will be there for me?
How can this be the life that I lead?

My side of the coin is a sleepless night
It's the fiery affliction in my chest
It's the loss of words and a touchless hand
I could fade silently away on a shore of sorrow
Or wage my roar in this purgatory
Don't you think I'd be the most befitting banshee
On my side of the coin;
I'd claw my heart out through my bones
Just for the chance to gift it to you
Lay to waste the framework that kept it safe
And run full scream ahead into potential
heartache again
I'm living and dying in fear with every sunrise
and set
All the words left unsaid
All the thoughts in my mind
Is it selfish of me to tell you my side of the coin
What if I'm where your heart belongs?
And you say I'm the only one
The nicest person you've ever met
That I'm someone you can't unlove
Would any of that be enough
To change the fate of a girl
On the wrong side of a coin

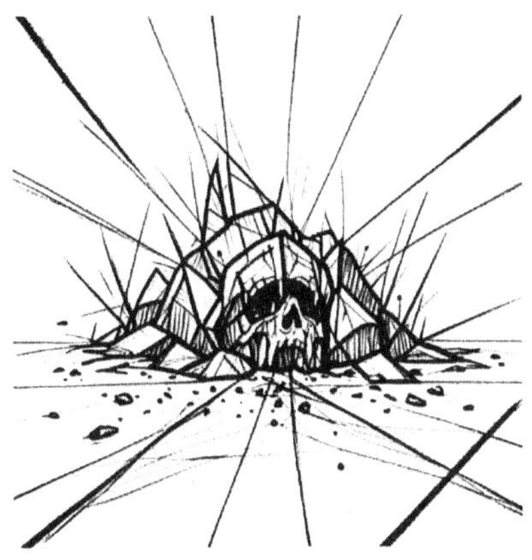

Sad Ass Title

It's just a bad day, just another sad day
Just another alone and empty feeling holiday
I'll coat them all with magic and present them
with a smile
I'll carry your insults and jabs on my own
I can handle another anger-thrown fight
Because the sun still shines even behind dark
clouds
Even when your demons try to snuff the light
out
Your laughter and support act like music to my
fears
You love bomb, I trudge along
As the most unenjoyable person that you have
ever met

Your infectious charisma paralyzes me
How can you always be so on?
How can you act like nothing's wrong?
But I can see you Jekyll and Hyde
I can feel your anger escaping from your pores
I hit the ground any chance I get
To shatter my knees and beg you please
Please hang up this cycle
I've never begged for anything more
Can't you hear me?
Can't you see me?
I'm a broken dinner plate scattered on the floor
Yet you cut yourself by your own hand
And attack me like I'm the enemy
Just be nice I'm on your side
I don't want you to turn into only Hyde
Let my cry be enough for you to see
How there has to be a change for us to survive
Fake it 'til ya make it only gets you so far
You can't avoid, lash out, rage and ignore
And expect me to stay forever
Chained to your temper
I'm a prisoner to your mood
The highs are alluring and oh so beautiful
But the lows terrorize and demonize
Grinding away at my lonely bones
Strangling all of my sunshine
And hollowing out my soul
I rewrite and reread and regret parts of our story

Pages torn and lovers scorn
A timeless tale of loving a man unwilling to seek
help
Too avoidant to understand the impact of his
words
That his continued storms will be the cause of
his truest hurt
I scoured this world for the brighter days
And took the darkness in stride
She's an angel they would say
But at some point that version of me died

Siren Screams

Play with my hair and just be here
No one has to know
You bring the snacks
And I'll bring the tears
We can at least find comfort in this night
Tell me we'll remain friends
Whenever whatever this is ends
I don't have it in me to not hurt you
So promise to protect yourself
And don't answer if I call
Don't let my siren song reach your ears
I'm not sure I can care enough to stop
I'd give in to company
Just to avoid being alone
I'm not one to indulge in selfishness
But with you I will, I know
You won't hesitate
And in this wretched state of mind
I'll use that to my advantage
Go ahead and make a deal
Sell your soul
Just for me to temporarily feel
There's nothing here for you to gain
No prize to show off
Just shadows condensed in the dark
Let my siren self consume your heart

An enchantress' encampment
Foolish enough to venture in
Brave enough to think you had something to win
I'd let you walk but you knew the risk
I've fallen victim to my role, altered my soul
I can hear my voice singing for you to be closer
Wreckage in the night
Hellbound with you
I am lost and found with you
I accept your emotional sacrifice
And raise you just one more encounter
Just one more night of total darkness
Then I'll leave you in a muddled wonder

Ladybug

I fail to recall how many times our paths have crossed
How many chances we mindlessly lost
I used to drench our names with hearts
The first boy I was convinced that I loved
A tender ache of lunchtime games
Long lost couples skate
Forbidden movie dates
My thumbprint memorized the pattern of your house number
Perpetually nervous to call
Whimsically ready to fall
I trust you with my deepest truths
And you heroically protect my every word
I swear you could've fixed any problem
With only your smile and a hug
I fold up our memories like I used to fold you notes
Sign each one with just a love drawn ladybug
Deny my hand, but I vow to wait
With an impatient heart and a stuttering spark
Kiss me when we grow up
And solidify our fate to be nothing more than a temporary high
A mislabeled pill on a momentary night

My most dramatic exit
How could you love someone you don't know
anymore
I break my own heart and choose the front door
You don't follow me into the street
Into the dark night air, packed with stale laughter
A numbing thing it is to be alone in a crowd of
friends
I know it's best to keep far away
But my bones won't allow me to give up
harboring this spark
Waiting for you to chat me UnderTheStars952
Because I never was able to voice aloud
That I always had that first undying love for you

A Man of Potential

I find that I'm attracted to things a little broken
A little blue
Broody by nature, maybe even a bit mean
But I'm a vial of sunshine
Surely I can help him if he's mine
I can make you feel brand new
If I'm giving and only focus on you
Sacrifice my time, my mind, my every hope
For the glimmer of potential I see
I'll fixate on the you I want you to be
I'll romanticize your every fiber
And fabricate a wonderous life
You know I'd make the most annoyingly positive
wife

Let me get lost in my fantasy
Let me believe the beautiful lies
That you never should've said to me
You're just an echo of my blissful thoughts
A lack of work in progress
A frozen hand on a broken clock
When I give you my all
Why must you make me feel pathetically small
Why can't you just admit
That you might actually be sick
Take my hand and I can light the way
But your stubborn mind won't put us first
Sew patches on you until my fingers bleed
Until I finally see there is no need
It's not a choice I can make for you
And this selfless life is drowning me
A fruitless effort
More give, more take
And you'll never change
Because you think you are fine
A mirage of a man I consistently ran to
A febrile fight against a heartbreak
That is fated to darken my sunshine soul
This is the tragedy that is my reality
I fell in love with a version of you
That never was or never will be true

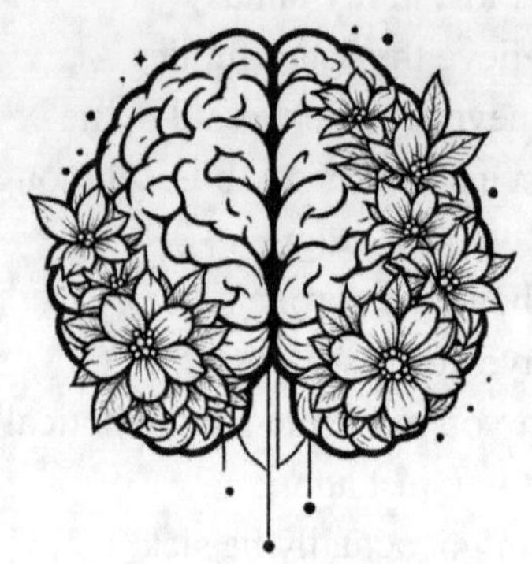

Post Love

Where are you
Just spill the tea
My curiosity is starting to eat away at me
How often do you think of us
Do you see my face climbing in your truck
Or singing country at the top of my lungs
My feet are muddied with memories of you
So much that I almost called
If I could just see your life now
I'd offer my veins in exchange
Transformed to a myth, I would wander
Ghostly and lonely and eyes asunder
Foraging for your tracks
I need you to want me but I don't want us back
I frequent the places we've been

And relive our every sin
A harrowing fixation
And a deadly demonstration
But what does it matter if I'm already your ghost
Who or what or when am I
I've seemed to have lost my sense of self
Time skips by as I drive to your house
Repeated with a glaze of familiarity
A post-love time warp
One day I might be brave enough to go up and
knock
To finally see your mom again
To hope she's up for a talk
For now your truck is always gone
Leaving me to believe you must've moved on
A feverish longing to know your truth
And an empty bed I made myself
I'd trace your steps if I knew where to start
Staying two feet behind to maybe quiet this
stalker heart

I Am My Teardrop

You compelled me to believe your words
That tears are weak and emotions are worse
But deep down I knew my truth
That tears only define my strength
Your lack of them might seal your fate
Don't underestimate what my tears can do
They reflect the beauty of this world
A wildflower in every drop
Dazzling and sparkling
They are my soul on display
My wonder and admiration made physical and
real
My tears hold sorrow
Earth shattering and soul scattering
A scream alone just would not do

They pour like a hurricane
Only uncomfortable to you
I know I'm a lot, I know I feel bone deep
Too easy to cry and too emotional to stop
But these tears are my lifeline to understand my
place
You'll never know the feeling of being
someone's true safe space
So go ahead and scream CRY in my face
Just because you're filled with rage
A beast you never learned to contain
You scathe and claw and rip away
At any ounce of happiness you might engage
You can't express and you can't hold back
Any hint of emotion is transcribed to mad
You'll beat me blue with the absence of apology
A missing wonder of the world
My tears were passion when I was fighting for
you
Begging you to pause and hear me out too
Sensitive I'll always be
A trait I've learned to love
It makes for a life of full experience
A human range we were born to indulge
I'm thankful to know I have an abundance of
tears
And will not waste another one on your selfish
self-loathing hopeless years

Ghosts

Until we are ghosts, I will be haunted by you
Spending my existence as your serenade on
standby
Knowing full well that the ridges of our
fingertips orchestrate a symphony exclusive to
our ears
I'll pace my day to the tempo of your heartbeat
Fill my thoughts with the scent of you
I could never be untouched by our gravity
Spin and kiss, revisit your laugh
When can I see you again
You try to take my wish back
An eyelash freefalling from your finger
But the wish is mine to keep
Even if you are the only one who can grant it
Abandon me
Bitten and bruised
Pleasure is pain and your pain is all I bare
Tighten this straight jacket
You're an I love you traced into the palm of my
hand
Engraved by you
I am tragically enslaved to you
Enlisted to this self-sabotaging suicide mission
Isolated now to a footnote of your bedsheets

But we were written to be unconditional,
ultimate sacrificial
A fatal farewell
Forced to trade a lifetime of your love for a plot
of degraded soil
Sowing my early grave
Why couldn't you be the one who got to stay
Who never got away
The one who got to love me
Until we are ghosts

My (guitar) Hero

It was innocent, but they will never believe us
Feeding our playful midnight energy
Your hands on the wheel, mine on your thigh
Wheel wells filled with pebbles
Come, climb into my room
Let's listen to the CD you made for me
I'll break into your garage to paint your car
Happy birthday to my lover
Every dance, every vacation, every frozen
two-strawed treat
You were the pure essence of a high-school
sweetheart
I'd never regret the day I reached for your hand
If I could, I'd live out memories of us again
To play guitar hero with you in my prom dress
And get your car stuck on the 4th of July
Let's make our own fireworks
We wrote the rules for future lovers
A cascade of moral endeavors
Painting swirls of beaches
A modern Picasso and Monet
It heartbreakingly wasn't enough for me to stay
Your drive like a contagion fueled my
inspiration

But I sold our art as the heathen of time tore us
apart
The only person who memorized and anticipated
my every move and thought
Kiss me three times but never just twice
I was foolish the day I declared you were too
nice

Twisted Roots

You wanted everything to be fair
But when things really mattered you didn't care
You tipped the scales to benefit yourself
To run the narrative
And run our house
Aggression runs deeper than I could ever believe
Your twisted tormented mindset
I wish it didn't have to demolish me
Challenge me to your life-size chess
And proudly display your false pretense
That even you thought were true
When will you understand
There is no winning
There is no final score to settle
Trash your fantasies of being better
With no motivation, only aggravation
You preach my perfection
But only to your continuous failures
Competition is only fun in games
You adopted it as a lifestyle
You gave a face to the name
And an end to your reign
Paint me however your heart desires
You finally won, You proved a point
Even if no one knows that point but you

An empty-handed heartless battle
No trophy or ribbon
But you felt you had something to prove
You sadly created this fight you had to "win"
You're wiser than a spider spinning an obvious
web
You grew a decaying system of roots
To pull the ground out from beneath me
All the while you remain standing

Booze Cruise

A Popov and Sunny D state of mind
The back roads were our domain
No rules or laws or sense of time
I still don't know how we didn't die
The greatest love story to ever unfold
At least that's how we recited it
They would ask if it was you and me
Not yet we'd say, but one day it will be
Our eyes full of want and conversation to match
No doubt the sands of time would steady our
pact
Patience, precision, timing
I fall custom to our banter
Come pick me up, let's chase tomorrow's sunrise
A midnight declaration
Screaming you belong with me
I'll leave my shoes, we can start a new adventure
Barefoot and free
Dancing shadows of these trees
I'll dig you out of your parent's house
If you dig me out of this ditch
We were written in the stars
Undeniable by even the most stubborn of hearts
I pledge to always sing I run to you

Absolutely no force of nature could keep us
apart
You drive, I pour
We sing, I want you more
Write me into the rest of your love songs
It's finally our time to be
Push and pull this gravity is in control
I surrender to the smallest advance
Show me what you want with a trace of your
hand
I'll save my breath to spend on you
Sink all my rules and let down my walls
To live my nights like we could have it all
Like life and love could never move on
But friends don't always make for lovers
My privilege to your late nights was revoked
I missed the train and you rode alone
Straight into my best friend's home
If thoughts were fatal, we would burn together
A reciprocating love triangle display
So I stumble headfirst into a rainstorm
Wash my feelings of you
And breathe again in the light of day
We diminished to only birthday texts
But even that has disappeared now too
You live fondly frozen in my mind
With my most reckless and invincible self
Of days we drank and nights we sang
A party bathroom makeout

Countless times of cruising fast
Knowing our time was stolen
I wouldn't choose nineteen to live with anyone
but you
We were positively golden

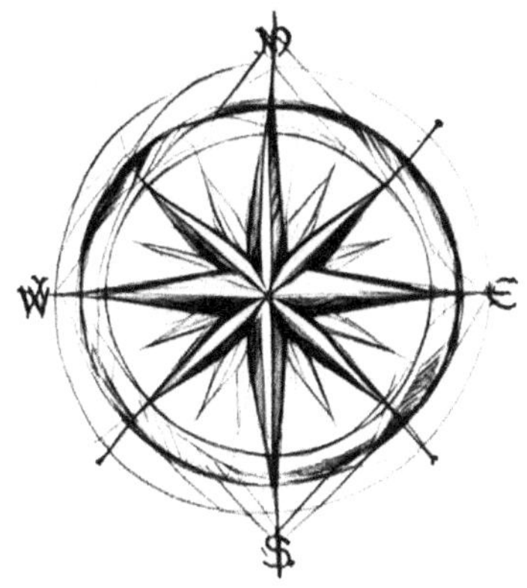

My Becoming

Litter the lawn with your clothes
Because I don't care if you ever come home
Ramble and rant
I'll flip this table
The same one you saw me dancing on
Your facade of cool fell to the ground
When you belittled my friends for fun
My cheeks are red, I hide but you seek
So I'll fake my strive for self-pride
And lock each door tonight
How dare you swear in my direction
A dialog you know I loathe
It's a grubby crime to disrespect my law
So I'll sprint aimlessly into the night
Smash my compass and blame it on you

A clumsy tumble and I have to return
Cuts wide open, with peroxide to burn
I faint and peek with one eye open
Someone come to my rescue
I haven't had enough attention
There is no replacement for these cravings
Savage and feisty, a wild thing no doubt
Learning to crawl with the shadows
A pit of hellfire I've become
The back and forth
Of this ruthless game we vowed to play
Whose crime was worse?
An absentee partner or the girl who cried wolf
What if one time I let you leave when you say I
deserve better
What if I know my worth, put myself first
Because my kind and caring side
I know I can turn that off
It would only take one time to stand up to you
Face my whimpering truth
I had a hand in making this messy bed
Just wait 'til I find my worth

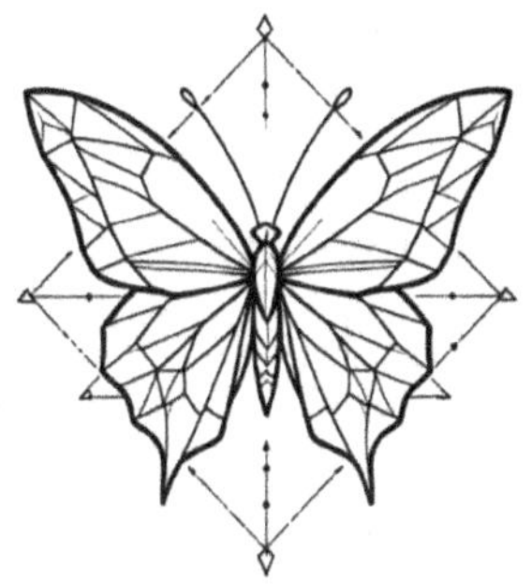

IYKYK

I've done it again
I never loved you, it was all a ruse
A song and dance choreographed by yours truly
Stitched you to my heart just to drag you
through the mud
I hope you felt every pebble, every bump
Started to drown in each pothole before I oh so
graciously pulled you out
Showed you a false reality in my kaleidoscope
of dreams
Your pathetic existence never mattered to me
I moved on effortlessly, abandoning you in the
dust
But your mind will never be allowed to escape
my escapades
Ohio isn't big enough for all my lovers
Midnight callers
Passing the time entertaining your friends

Dancing in the dark each night to the beat of a
new heart
No method to this madness
No need to walk with grace
I'm living my best lies…
Or maybe I've wiped away enough tears to
permanently prune my fingertips
Showing off wrinkles of my fragmented mind
Maybe I have a death grip on my independence
because it's all I have to embrace
Killing spiders, starting fires
Retreating to the pages of a long forgotten
journal
An ink blot drenched future turned to watercolor
wishes
Discovered the key to the shackles that held me
back
Falling in love with my personality
And weaving my life with beauty it used to lack
Maybe I've surrounded myself with the kindness
of my best friends
Spending nights running or reading
Maybe I realized too much time has passed since
I last stood barefoot in the rain
Allowed myself to feel and heal, to let go of all
this pain
I suppose the truth is as good as anyone's guess
But I hope you continue to gossip, I can't wait to
hear what I do next

Always More

There will never be so little of me that I am
unable to give more
No ounce of my skin and bone will go ungifted
if you ask
A gargoyle left in the rain to deter storms from
spoiling our fresh mortar
Spelling away any force that could tarnish my
idea of you
Storm chased by storm
Concrete feet weigh me down
Cast to the exterior, positioned to be excluded
Still optimistic of your presence
Decline any plans at the thought of the chance to
see your face
Drop anything I'm in the middle of

Rearrange my days in case we get to speak
Too busy dreaming to sleep at night
Rip my door from the hinges to make sure you
know it is always open
That I alone could fill your cup
Be the one to always show up
Make sure your every wish comes true
I will choose you first as long as I live
My only thought remains
As I stand with exposed bones
That there is no end to what I can give

Your Psycho Ex-Lover

You offered a hug, and I couldn't bring myself
to be the one to let go first
I had never felt nervous around you before
This time I was; Why?
Because you were in control of what happens
next
Because your body called for mine to be close
And I was... helplessly close
I felt everything
The familiarity of our bodies pressed together
The softness in your hands caressing my back
The comfort of your head resting on mine
The silent intimacy that we have always known
My hand made its way to your collarbone
And your hand to my hair
And when I finally stepped back I touched your
face
And fell into the depths of your eyes
Like I have so many times before
I hesitated to kiss you and forced myself to look
away
But you stopped holding back
You kissed me like you had no choice but to
give in
And with that, I melted into you

Allowing my soul to flow effortlessly into you
And now I am unapologetically yours
Waiting for you to embrace that you'll always be
mine

Xoxo, Your Psycho Ex-Lover

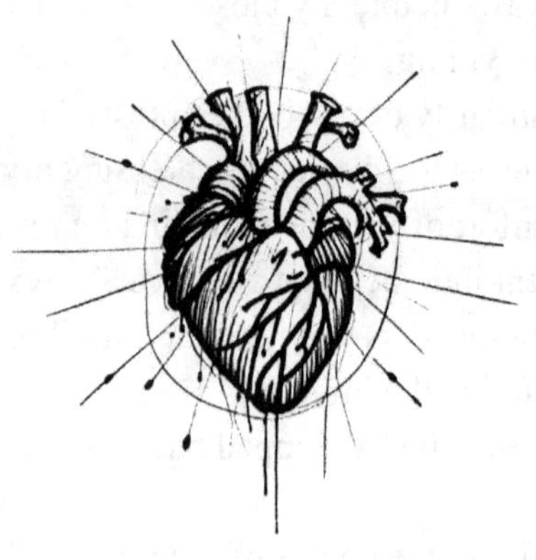